A DAY IN THE LIFE OF A
FIREFIGHTER

THIS EDITION

Produced for DK by WonderLab Group LLC
Jennifer Emmett, Erica Green, Kate Hale, *Founders*

Editor Maya Myers; **Photography Editor** Nicole DiMella; **Managing Editor** Rachel Houghton;
Designers Project Design Company; **Researcher** Michelle Harris; **Copy Editor** Lori Merritt;
Indexer Connie Binder; **Proofreader** Susan K. Hom; **Series Reading Specialist** Dr Jennifer Albro

This edition published in 2025
First published in Great Britain in 2025 by
Dorling Kindersley Limited
20 Vauxhall Bridge Road,
London SW1V 2SA

The authorised representative in the EEA is
Dorling Kindersley Verlag GmbH. Arnulfstr. 124,
80636 Munich, Germany

A CIP catalogue record for this book
is available from the British Library.
ISBN: 978-0-2417-1858-2

Printed and bound in China

Super Readers Lexile® levels 310L to 490L
Lexile® is the registered trademark of MetaMetrics, Inc. Copyright © 2024 MetaMetrics, Inc. All rights reserved.

The publisher would like to thank the following for their kind permission to reproduce their images:
a=above; c=centre; b=below; l=left; r=right; t=top; b/g=background

123RF.com: Jamroen Jaiman 17b; **Alamy Stock Photo:** Ira Berger 6br, 30clb, FirePhoto 29, Marmaduke St. John 9,
Niels Kliim 18, 30cl, PA Images / Jane Barlow 19tr, PA Images / Lewis Whyld 24, Art Phaneuf 22, Felix Shoughi 6-7;
Dreamstime.com: Colorfuelstudio 26cl, 26clb, Itrashm 23cr, Montree Lakchit 13crb, Monkey Business Images 3,
10-11, Tina Nizova 26bl, Tyler Olson 14t, Leonid Smirnov 16, Thomas L Spetter 1, Serhii Suravikin 12, 30bl, Victor
Torres 20-21; **Getty Images:** Moment / Lepretre Pierre 8; **Getty Images / iStock:** AlenaPaulus 21tr, E+ / Andresr
28b, E+ / Birzio 4-5, E+ / Dlewis33 28c, E+ / Kali9 17t, E+ / LPETTET 25t, E+ / Xavierarnau 9cr, EvgeniyShkolenko
25cr, Jesus Rodriguez 11, Tampatra 23b; **Shutterstock.com:** Colorfuel Studio 26cla, Erikjohnphotography 7bl,
30cla, Liangchaochao 13t, Pipas Imagery 14-15b, 30tl, Yiistocking 19cla; **U.S. Air National Guard:** Senior Master
Sgt. Vincent De Groot 7br; **U.S. Fire Administration:** 27

Cover images: *Front:* **Dreamstime.com:** Applikbeats777 (Background); **Shutterstock.com:** Tara Lambourne,
Fluke Samed ca/ (Texture); *Back:* **Dreamstime.com:** Abscent clb, Oleksandr Bolotov cra

www.dk.com

MIX
Paper | Supporting
responsible forestry
FSC™ C018179

This book was made with Forest
Stewardship Council™ certified
paper – one small step in DK's
commitment to a sustainable future.
**Learn more at www.dk.com/uk/
information/sustainability**

A DAY IN THE LIFE OF A

FIREFIGHTER

Paige Towler

Contents

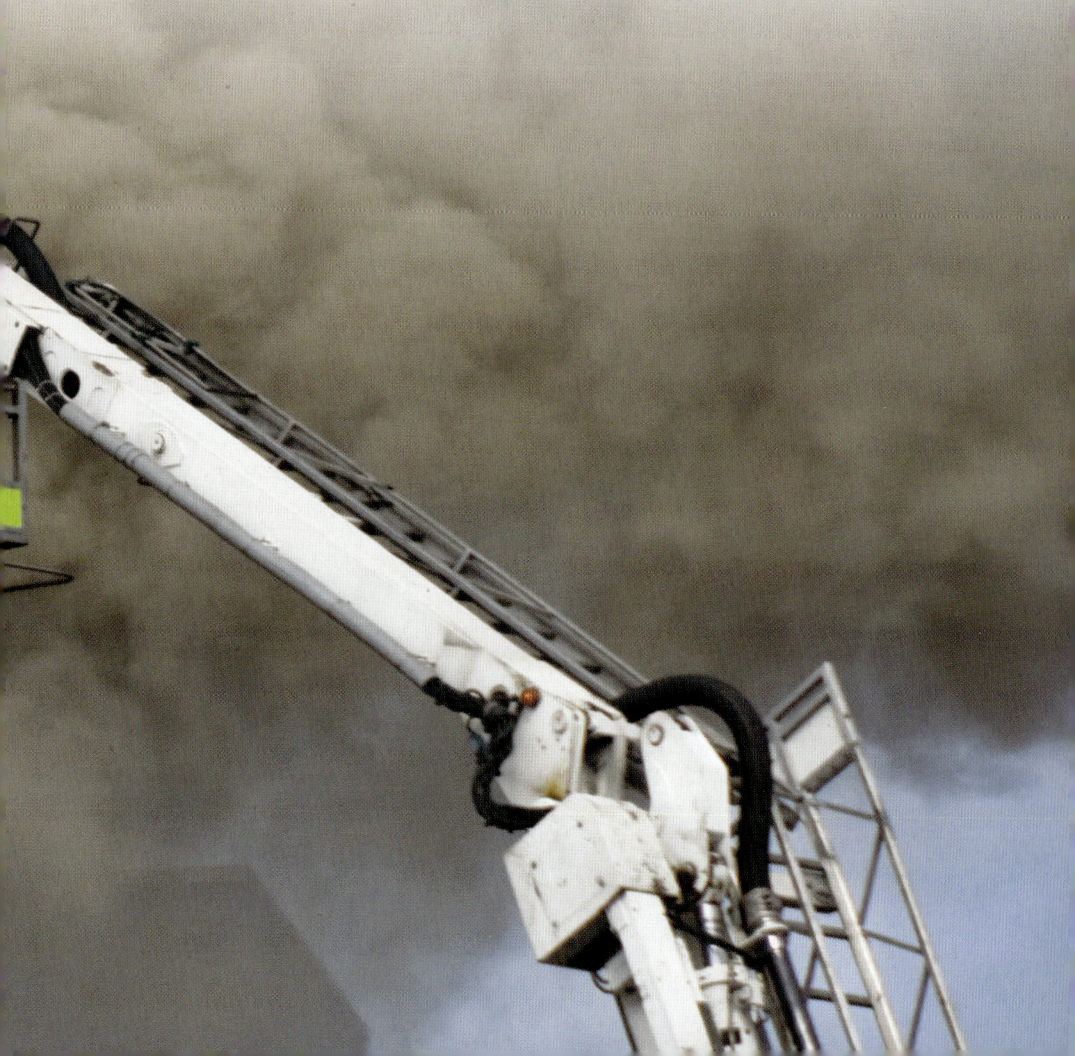

Meet a Firefighter

Oh no! A building is on fire! Who can help? A firefighter.

A firefighter's job is to help to keep people safe. Firefighters are trained to put out fires. They also help people who are unwell or hurt.

Firefighters are called first responders. They respond to emergencies.

Firefighters wake up bright and early. They get to the fire station on time. They put on their uniform. Firefighters wear trousers and shirts. These are easy to move in.

Time to go to work!

Firefighters work in turns called shifts. A shift can last for up to 24 hours. That's one whole day! A shift can be busy or quiet.

The station manager is in charge at the station. The station manager tells the firefighters what to do.

Getting Ready

Gear keeps a firefighter safe. Firefighters wear thick trousers and heavy coats. These are made out of cloth that is hard to burn.

Firefighters wear boots with thick soles. They wear a helmet.

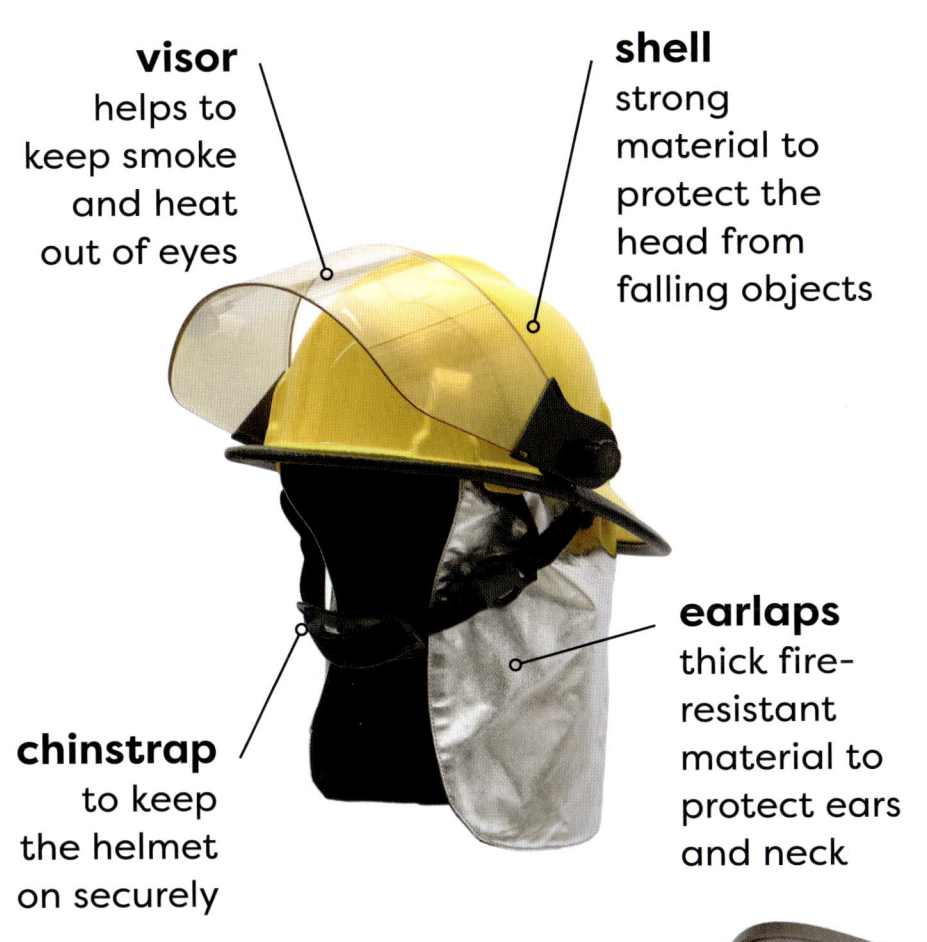

visor
helps to keep smoke and heat out of eyes

shell
strong material to protect the head from falling objects

earlaps
thick fire-resistant material to protect ears and neck

chinstrap
to keep the helmet on securely

They use special masks called respirators. These help firefighters to breathe when there is smoke from a fire.

fire hose

Next, the firefighters check the fire engine. The engine is the truck they take to an emergency.

The firefighters make sure the engine is working. They check the ladder. They check the fire hose. They test the lights. They make sure the tyres are full of air. Ready!

Firefighters have other important tools. This is their equipment. They must check this, too.

A firefighter checks the medical bag. Firefighters often have to help people who are ill or hurt.

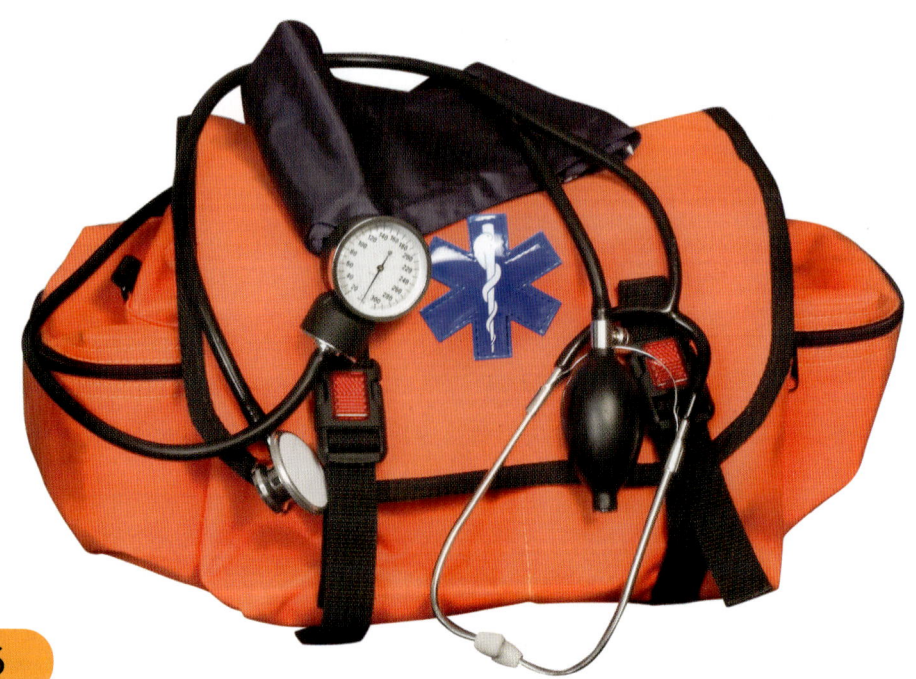

This firefighter has an axe. An axe can help to cut down beams or walls that are in the way.
All set!

On Call

Now the firefighters are on call. They are ready to help with an emergency.

While they are waiting for a call, firefighters practise. This is called training. Firefighters need to be strong. They need to be fast. They need to know how to use their gear.

Fire!

A call comes in. There is a fire! Time to go!

The firefighters get into the engine. They turn on flashing lights. They turn on the siren. Other cars move out of the way.

A building is on fire. The firefighters grab the fire hose. They spray water over the fire.

Firefighters make sure everyone is out of the building. They keep everyone safe.

Finally, the fire goes out!

Helping Out

Firefighters do more than put out fires. They help with other emergencies, too.

Sometimes, people can get ill or hurt. Firefighters are there to help. They work to keep people and animals safe.

Firefighters teach people about fire safety. They show people how to stay safe.

If there is a fire:

 **Call 999** right away.

 Stay low to avoid smoke.

 Get away from the fire and stay away.

 Leave the building if you can.

Firefighters tell people how to prevent fires. They warn people to never play with matches or lighters.

They also teach people to use smoke alarms. These alarms warn you when there is smoke from a fire.

Sleeping at the Station

It is hard work being a firefighter! It has been a long day. The firefighters cook dinner together. They eat at the station.

Emergencies can happen at night, too. Firefighters sleep at the station. They sleep in beds called bunks. Tomorrow, they will wake up early again. Good night!

Glossary

fire engine
a truck used
by firefighters

fire hose
a strong hose that
sprays a lot of water

fire station
the place where a
firefighter works

first responder
a person who is
trained to help
during emergencies

gear
clothing and equipment
that keeps a firefighter
safe

Index

Quiz

Answer the questions to see what you have learned. Check your answers with an adult.

1. How long can a firefighter's shift last?

2. Name one part of the fire engine.

3. Why is a firefighter's gear important?

4. True or False: A firefighter has to be ready when they are on call.

5. How does a firefighter keep people safe?

1. 24 hours 2. Ladder, siren, lights, tyres 3. It keeps them safe.
4. True 5. Putting out fires, helping ill or hurt people, teaching about fire safety.